THE LIFE OF MARY

Nihil Obstat: Right Reverend Archimandrite Francis Vivona, S.T.M., J.C.L.
Imprimatur: Most Reverend Joseph A. Pepe, D.D., J.C.D.
Date: August 12, 2014

By Bart Tesoriero
Illustrated by Miguel D. Lopez

catholic
children's
CLASSICS

ISBN 978-1-61796-140-3

Artwork and Text © 2014 Aquinas Kids, Phoenix, Arizona
Second Printing, July, 2018
Printed in China

Adam and Eve

A long, long time ago, God made the heavens and the earth. He made the sun and the moon, the trees and plants, and all the creatures of the earth. God wanted a family, so He created Adam and Eve and put them in a beautiful Garden!

God told Adam and Eve that they could eat of the fruit of every tree in the Garden except for the tree of the knowledge of good and evil. He told them that if they ate that fruit, they would die. The devil, in the form of a serpent, told Adam and Eve that if they ate the fruit of that tree, they would become like God. Adam and Eve disobeyed God and ate the fruit. Sadly, they lost God's presence in their hearts.

Our first parents could no longer stay in the Garden. However, God still loved them. He promised to send a Redeemer to save all people. He said the Redeemer would be born of a woman, who would crush the head of the serpent.

Many years passed. God chose Abraham to be the father of the Jews, God's chosen people. Over many years and through many trials, God slowly prepared His people for the coming of the Redeemer. He led them out of Egypt into a country all their own, a holy land named Israel. They waited patiently for God to keep His promise and to send the Redeemer, whom they called the Messiah.

Joachim and Anne

Many years after Abraham, there lived in Israel an elderly couple named Joachim and Anne. They were sad because they had no children. They trusted in God and continued to pray and serve others. God heard their prayers. Anne conceived in her womb a daughter, Mary. Through God's amazing favor and grace, Mary was conceived without Original Sin.

Anne cared tenderly and joyfully for her little daughter Mary. She felt deeply blessed by the presence of her pure and lovely child. Joachim and Anne's home was filled with peace and grace.

From the time she was a little girl, Mary loved to help others. She fed the birds and cared for the little creatures that played in her yard. When she grew older, Mary helped her mother to cook and bake. Sometimes Mary and her mother and father would walk outside together to enjoy the beautiful warm sun and the cool breezes blowing across the hills of Nazareth.

Mary played happily with her little friends. Everyone in Nazareth especially loved her bright eyes and her cheerful smile.

People felt better around
Mary, although they did not
really know why. She brought
joy wherever she went.

5

Joseph and Mary

Joseph was a strong and quiet young carpenter who had lived in Nazareth his whole life. His ancestor was King David, the most famous king of Israel, who lived about 1,000 years before Joseph was born.

Joseph worked hard building and repairing homes for the people of Nazareth. He made doors and windows, beds, tables, and chairs.

One day a friend told Joseph about a beautiful young woman named Mary, whom he had seen with the other young ladies at the well in Nazareth. "Go meet her!" his friend said. "I think it will mean something good!" So Joseph went down to the well, and there he met the lovely young Mary. She was modest, yet very kind. Joseph offered to carry her water jar for her, and they became friends.

As the days passed into months, Joseph and Mary fell in love with each other and became engaged. According to the custom, they were considered man and wife even though they did not yet live together. However, the most amazing event in history was soon to change their lives forever!

The Annunciation

One day, not long after Joseph and Mary were engaged, God sent the angel Gabriel to Mary. The angel said, "Hail, Mary, full of grace! The Lord is with you." Mary was surprised to see the angel, and she thought to herself, "What sort of greeting is this?"

The angel continued, "Do not be afraid, Mary, for God is very pleased with you. Behold, you will conceive a son in your womb and you shall name him Jesus. He will be great. People will call him the Son of the Most High, and God will give him the throne of David his father. His kingdom will last forever."

Mary asked the angel, "How can this be, since I am a virgin?" The angel replied, "The Holy Spirit will come upon you, and the power of the Most High will overshadow you. Therefore the child to be born will be called the Son of God." Mary answered, "Behold, I am the handmaid of the Lord. Let it be done unto me according to your word."

Soon afterwards, an angel told Joseph in a dream, "Do not be afraid to take Mary your wife into your home. She will bear a son and you are to name him Jesus, for he will save his people from their sins."

Jesus is Born!

Months passed, and Mary was ready to give birth. The Roman Emperor had commanded everyone to return to the towns where they were born to be counted. Joseph and Mary left Nazareth and made the long journey to Bethlehem, where King David had been born.

It was late when they arrived in Bethlehem, and Mary was very tired. Joseph found a little stable, with a manger in it, where the animals were fed. That night Mary gave birth to her son, Jesus. Mary wrapped her new baby in warm clothing and laid him in the manger, where it was warm.

There were shepherds watching over their flocks in the fields that night. Suddenly, an angel of the Lord came to them in a bright light, saying, "Do not be afraid! I bring you good news of great joy: Today in the city of David a savior is born for you who is Messiah and Lord. This will be a sign for you: you will find a baby lying in a manger."

The shepherds arose quickly and ran to the stable, where they found Mary and Joseph, and the baby lying in the manger. They told Mary and Joseph about the angels and their message.

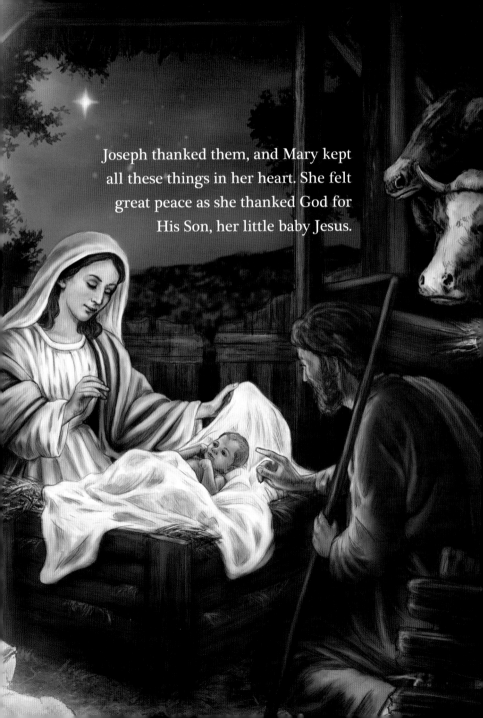

Joseph thanked them, and Mary kept all these things in her heart. She felt great peace as she thanked God for His Son, her little baby Jesus.

The Presentation of Jesus in the Temple

Forty days after Jesus was born, Joseph and Mary took him to the temple in Jerusalem to present him to the Lord.

A holy old man named Simeon lived in Jerusalem. He loved God very much. The Holy Spirit had promised Simeon that he would not die until he had seen the Redeemer of the Lord.

On that day the Spirit inspired Simeon to come into the Temple. When he saw Joseph, Mary, and Jesus, Simeon took the child into his arms. He blessed God, saying,

"Now, Master, you may let your servant go
in peace, according to Your word,
for my eyes have seen Your salvation,
which you prepared in sight of all the nations:
a light for the Gentiles,
and glory for Your people Israel."

Simeon blessed Mary and Joseph. He then said to Mary, "This child will cause many in Israel to fall and rise. He shall be a sign that many will not accept. A sword shall pierce your own soul, so that the thoughts of many hearts may be revealed."

At Home in Nazareth

In time, Joseph and his little family returned to Nazareth. Mary cared for them with all the love in her heart. She rose early every day to prepare breakfast, and worked hard cooking, cleaning, spinning, and going to the well!

God had commanded His Jewish people to celebrate the Passover feast every year. They remembered how God had delivered them from Egypt. When Jesus was twelve years old, the family went up to Jerusalem for the feast. After it was over, they returned to Nazareth, but Jesus remained behind, without his parents knowing it.

Joseph and Mary returned to Jerusalem to look for Jesus. Finally, after three days they found him in the temple, listening to the teachers and priests and asking them questions. Everyone who heard Jesus was surprised.

Mary said, "Son, why have you done this to us?" Jesus answered, "Did you not know I must be in my Father's house?" Mary and Joseph did not understand his answer.

Jesus went back home with his parents to Nazareth, and he obeyed them. Mary kept all the words of Jesus in her heart.

Meanwhile, Jesus grew in
wisdom, age, and favor before
God and all the people.

15

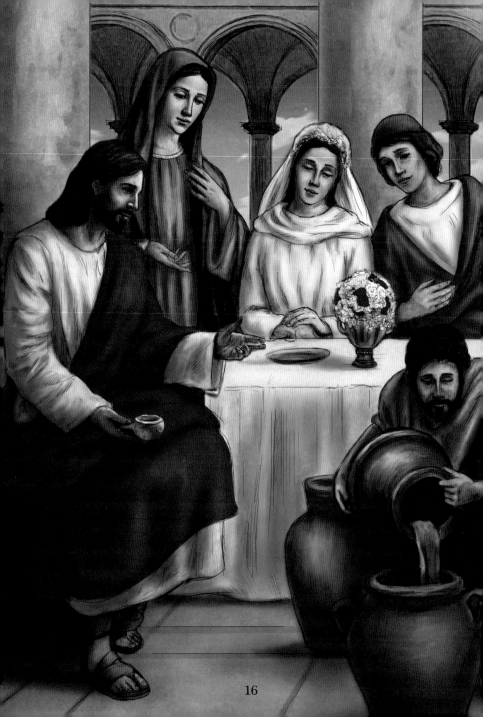

The Wedding at Cana

When Jesus was 30 years old, he was baptized by John the Baptist. Afterwards, the Spirit led him into the desert to be tested. He returned, filled with the Holy Spirit and the power of God, and news of him began to spread.

There was a wedding in the little town of Cana, and the family invited Mary and Jesus and his friends to attend. The guests drank up the wine, and Mary said to Jesus, "They have no wine." Jesus replied, "My hour has not yet come." Mary told the servers, "Do whatever he tells you."

Jesus told the servants to fill six large stone jars with water. Jesus then said, "Give some to the headwaiter." The servants did as he told them. The headwaiter tasted the water, which had become wine. He then called the bridegroom over and said, "Usually people serve the good wine first, and then, when people have drunk a lot, they serve the lesser wine. But you have kept the good wine until now."

When the disciples of Jesus saw this miracle, they began to believe in him. Mary was thankful her son had done this miracle, but she knew it was now time for him to leave her and to begin his work of healing and teaching.

Mary Stands Beneath the Cross

For three years Jesus served the people of Israel, healing and teaching them about his heavenly Father. Some of the rulers did not believe that Jesus was God's Son. They arrested Jesus. They took him to Pilate, the Roman governor. Pilate had his soldiers beat Jesus and crown him with thorns. Then he condemned Jesus to death.

Jesus carried a heavy cross to a hill called Calvary. Many people shouted at Jesus and made fun of him. As Jesus walked on the way, Mary came to be with him. She felt very sorrowful in her heart to see her son suffer. She knew that he loved us so much that he was willing to die for us.

When they reached the top of the hill, the soldiers nailed Jesus to the cross. Mary and John, one of Jesus' apostles, stood beneath the cross in silent prayer. Mary and Jesus gazed at each other with great love. Jesus said to Mary, "Woman, behold your son." Then he said to John, "Behold your mother." In this way, Jesus gave Mary to us as our mother also. Then Jesus bowed His head and died.

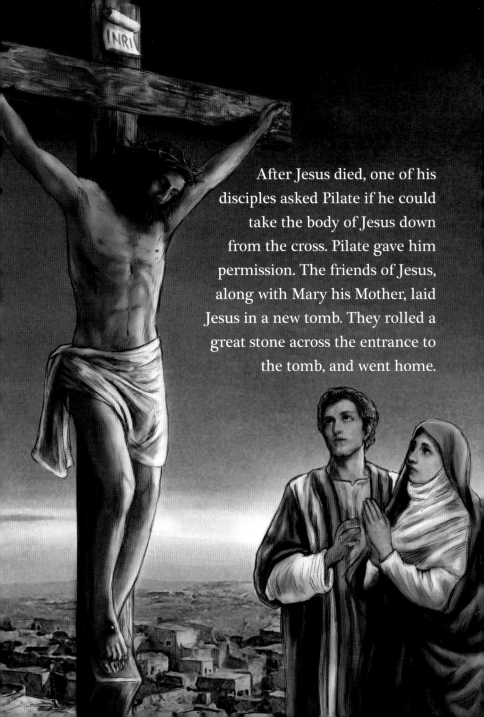

After Jesus died, one of his disciples asked Pilate if he could take the body of Jesus down from the cross. Pilate gave him permission. The friends of Jesus, along with Mary his Mother, laid Jesus in a new tomb. They rolled a great stone across the entrance to the tomb, and went home.

Mary Remembers Her Son

At home, Mary sat quietly, thinking back over the years. She remembered what it was like on that cold night in Bethlehem when she gave birth to Jesus. She remembered the shepherds visiting them, with their scruffy little sheep. She thought of the Magi, the Wise Men, who had come with gifts of gold and spices for the newborn King.

Mary remembered going with Joseph to present Jesus to God in the temple, and how old Simeon had told her that a sword of sorrow would pierce her heart. She began to weep, as she thought of Jesus playing around the house as a little boy. She remembered how Joseph loved to take Jesus on walks, and to hike the hills around Nazareth. She smiled as she thought of them working together in the carpenter shop. Jesus loved working with his father!

Mary thought about all that Jesus had done to help his people. She remembered how he taught them about God and how to love God as a Father. She thought of all the people he had healed, the blind, the deaf, and the lame.

"Dear God," Mary prayed, "thank You for choosing me to bear Your Son. It was so hard to see him suffer and die for all of us, Your children. But this is Your Will. You love us all so much that You gave us Your only Son."

Jesus Rises from the Dead!

Early in the morning on the first day of the week, the Roman soldiers who guarded the tomb of Jesus were startled. They felt the ground move beneath their feet. They looked up in fear as an angel came down from heaven and rolled away the stone from the tomb. Suddenly in a burst of great light, Jesus arose from the dead! The soldiers ran away as fast as they could.

Many people believe that Jesus first went to see His mother Mary. She had been with Him all His life, and had stayed with Him when He was on the cross. Surely He would first visit Mary when He arose in glory!

Just after sunrise, Mary Magdalene and some women came to the tomb to anoint the body of Jesus. "The stone is rolled away! Where is Jesus?" they cried. The angel said to them, "Do not be afraid! He is not here, for He is risen, just as He said. Come and see the place where He lay."

The women left the tomb quickly. They were very excited, and they ran to tell the good news to Peter and the other disciples. While they were on their way, Jesus Himself greeted them! The women bowed down to worship Him.

Jesus said to them, "Do not be afraid. Go tell My brothers to go to Galilee, and there they will see Me."

23

Pentecost

Jesus stayed on the earth for 40 days after His Resurrection. He appeared to His followers many times. He prepared His mother Mary and His apostles to continue bringing His Kingdom to all people. Jesus told them, "Do not leave Jerusalem, but wait there. In a few days you will receive power, when the Holy Spirit comes upon you. Then you will be My witnesses to the ends of the earth." When Jesus had said this, He blessed His Mother and His disciples, and went up into heaven.

Mary and the apostles returned to an upper room in Jerusalem. Ten days later, the day of Pentecost came. Suddenly they heard a noise like a strong wind, which filled the whole room. They looked up, and saw tongues that looked like fire, which rested on each one of them. They were all filled with the Holy Spirit, and began to praise God in different tongues.

Peter stood up and proclaimed to all the people the good news that God had raised Jesus from the dead. Many of them repented of their sins and were baptized. God now had a new family, the Church, the people who believed in Jesus. God called Saint Paul to preach the Gospel to all people, and many more people joined the Church.

Mary is Taken Up to Heaven

In the days after Pentecost, Mary prayed for the apostles and helped the new believers as the Church began to grow. Just as Mary had helped prepare her own Son for His work on earth, so she helped His disciples.

Finally the time came for Mary to leave this earth. She missed Jesus very much. When Mary's life was over, God took her, both body and her soul, into heaven. Mary embraced her Son Jesus with great love. Jesus led her to a beautiful throne next to His own throne. She had suffered with Him on earth, and now she would live with Him in joy forever.

Jesus crowned Mary as the Queen of all the angels and saints. She is the Queen of heaven and earth. Mary continues to love us as our Mother in heaven. She helps us when we need her and whenever we pray for her aid. She wants to help all of us to feel God's love in our hearts and to please Him.

It is good for us to pray every day to Mary. When we feel afraid, she helps us to feel strong. When we feel sad, she helps us to feel joy. When we feel selfish, she helps us to serve others. She wants to help us get to heaven, to live forever with God our Father, Jesus, and the Holy Spirit.

Daily Prayers to Mary

Hail Mary

Hail Mary, full of grace, the Lord is with thee.
Blessed art thou among women,
and blessed is the fruit of thy womb, Jesus.

Holy Mary,
Mother of God,
pray for us sinners,
now and at the hour of our death. Amen.

Daily Consecration to Mary

O Mary, my Queen and my Mother,
I give myself entirely to you.
As proof of my devotion,
I consecrate to you this day,
my eyes, my ears, my mouth, my heart,
my whole being without reserve.

Wherefore, good Mother,
as I am your own,
keep me and guard me
as your property and possession. Amen.

Hail, Holy Queen

Hail, Holy Queen, Mother of Mercy,
Our life, our sweetness, and our hope!
To thee do we cry,
poor banished children of Eve;
to thee do we send up our sighs,
mourning and weeping in this valley of tears.
Turn then, most gracious advocate,
thine eyes of mercy towards us;
and after this our exile, show unto us
the blessed fruit of thy womb, Jesus;
O clement, O loving, O sweet Virgin Mary.

The Memorare

Remember, O most gracious Virgin Mary,
that never was it known, that anyone who fled
to thy protection, implored thy help,
or sought thy intercession, was left unaided.
Inspired by this confidence,
I fly unto thee, O Virgin of virgins my Mother.
To thee do I come, before thee I stand,
sinful and sorrowful. O Mother of the Word Incarnate,
despise not my petitions,
but in thy mercy hear and answer me. Amen.